G000129010

TUDOR

SECRETS

&

SCANDALS

IMPORTANT DATES

1485 Victory at Bosworth for Henry Tudor sees him crowned King Henry VII of England.

1509 Henry VIII becomes King of England.

1533 Henry VIII divorces Queen Catherine of Aragon to marry Anne Boleyn.

1540 Henry VIII divorces Anne of Cleves and marries Catherine Howard.

1547 Henry VIII is succeeded by his son, Edward VI.

1558 Elizabeth I becomes Queen of England.

1560s Religious wars take place in Europe between Protestants and Catholics.

1580 Francis Drake and his crew return to England after sailing around the world.

1587 Mary Queen of Scots is executed.

1603 Elizabeth I dies and James VI of Scotland becomes James I of England.

1503 James IV of Scotland marries Margaret Tudor, daughter of Henry VII.

1517 German priest Martin Luther sparks the Protestant Reformation.

1534 The Act of Supremacy makes Henry VIII head of the English Church.

1542 James V dies and his infant daughter becomes Mary Queen of Scots.

1553 Mary I becomes England's queen.

1561 Mary Queen of Scots returns to Scotland from France.

1567 The future James VI of Scotland is born; his father Lord Darnley is murdered.

1586 The Babington Plot to murder Elizabeth I is uncovered.

1588 The English fleet defeat the Spanish Armada; England's war with Spain lasts until 1603.

▶▶ The Procession of Queen Elizabeth I by Robert Peake the Elder. (By kind permission of Mr J.K. Wingfield Digby, Sherborne Castle)

INTRODUCTION

The Tudors ruled England from 1485 until 1603, theirs an age of many secrets and frequent scandals. The rack and the gallows, the assassin's knife, potions and poisons, backstairs intrigue, scheming lords and maligned mistresses, alchemy and magic, science and superstition, religious wars and buccaneering exploration on the high seas – Tudor life was a heady brew, a vibrant time of adventure, change and danger, from the glittering court to the seamy underworld. The crowns of Tudor England and Stuart Scotland rested uneasily, and few close to the throne slept without cares. Today's heroes were often tomorrow's villains, for scandal, treason, misplaced trust or a secret laid bare could tumble the highest to the block or the hangman's rope.

UNEASY LIES THE HEAD

The Tudor dynasty seized the throne of England in 1485, when Henry, son of Edmund Tudor, became King Henry VII and ended the long Wars of the Roses. Yet in peace the new regime was insecure and the air thick with rumour and intrigue. Neither ally nor enemy could be trusted and there were many dark secrets – the darkest surrounding the vanished Princes in the Tower, the young sons of Edward IV. The new king's crown rested uneasily, for dark secrets were hidden in the candlelit corridors of power.

SECRETS OF THE CAR PARK

The Tudor victor paid scant respect to his defeated rival: after Richard III lost his crown and his life in the Battle of Bosworth, his corpse was stripped and mutilated and buried in the priory of Grey Friars in Leicester. But the priory was destroyed in 1538 and it was long believed that the royal bones ended up in the river. However, in 2012 a grave was found by archaeologists, beneath a Leicester car park, and DNA evidence (from the lineage of Richard's sister) confirmed the remains as those of Richard III. Forensic evidence indicated he had one shoulder higher than the other, hence his nickname 'crookback', and also how he died, one of several battlefield blows slicing off part of his skull. Richard was given a royal reburial, but his reputation remains contentious.

▲ The bones of Richard III, discovered in a car park in Leicester
© University of Leicester.

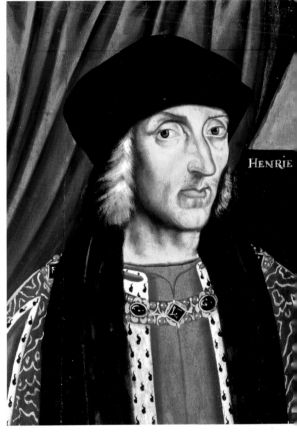

▲ Henry VII, the first of the Tudor monarchs of England (painting c.1626).

HENRY AND THE PRETENDERS

Having seized the crown in battle, Henry feared Yorkist counter-revolution. Edward IV's sons (the Princes in the Tower) had 'disappeared' and Richard III's only son had died aged 10 in 1484. The late king's nephew Warwick (son of the executed Duke of Clarence) was locked away. When a baker's son of the same age called Lambert Simnel appeared pretending to be Warwick 'escaped to Ireland', Henry displayed the real Warwick briefly in London to scotch the rumours. Simnel was crowned 'Edward VI' in Dublin and with a small army crossed to England, to be defeated in June 1487 near Newark. Henry scornfully sent the failed pretender to work, first in the kitchens, then as a falconer.

Ten years later another 'Warwick' appeared; Ralph Wilford was executed in February 1499, along with the friar who had taught him to impersonate Warwick. A more serious threat was posed by the Fleming Perkin Warbeck, claiming to be one of the Princes in the Tower and calling himself 'Richard IV'. After Warbeck's armed uprising in 1495 fizzled out, he was treated surprisingly gently, kept under house arrest at court until 1498, when he tried to escape. He was put in the stocks and forced to confess. A second escape plan in 1499, involving the hapless Warwick, was a gamble too far, and in November that year Perkin Warbeck was hanged at Tyburn. Warwick's short, unhappy life as a royal prisoner ended weeks later, also on the scaffold.

ROYAL LADIES

Young, highborn women were sent to court to advance their social standing and attract wealthy husbands. A maid of honour was young and single; a lady in waiting usually married and sometimes rich in her own right (such as Bess of Hardwick). Court ladies provided companionship and 'back office' help for the queen – and diversion for the king and his courtiers. Some secretly, or openly, became royal mistresses.

▼ The murder of the two Princes in the Tower.

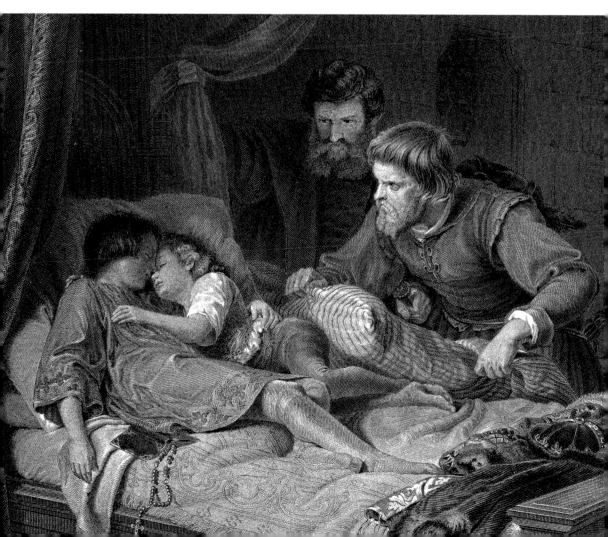

HENRY AND CATHERINE

The open secret of royal success was to remove rivals and sire sons, preferably with a spouse who brought diplomatic gains to the marriage bed. Henry VII's eldest son Prince Arthur married Spain's Princess Catherine of Aragon in 1501 – a useful match – but Arthur died a year later. Spain demanded the repayment of Catherine's dowry, but Henry, ever parsimonious, kept the money: he considered marrying the princess himself, since his wife Elizabeth of York died in 1503, but instead he betrothed her to his younger son Henry, then 11.

Henry VIII became king in 1509 and married Catherine. There seemed to be no scandals or secrets: the young king was handsome, talented, full of promise. Civil war memories were fading, the murky past rewritten in a politically correct pro-Tudor light. While Henry dreamed of military glory, his pressing need was a son. Great was his joy when Catherine became pregnant, but the infant (a boy born on New Year's Day 1511) died within two months. Four more pregnancies produced only one healthy child, a daughter, the future Queen Mary I.

▲ Catherine of Aragon, whose brief marriage to Prince Arthur had international repercussions.

◄ Arthur, Prince of Wales, son of Henry VII. Drawing from the north window of Jesus Chapel, Priory Church, Great Malvern.

GETTING A SON

In 1519 Henry fathered a son; unfortunately, the mother was not the queen, but the king's mistress Elizabeth ('Bessie') Blount. Bessie was a notable beauty, who came from Shropshire to be maid of honour to Queen Catherine. When the affair began, around 1515, Bessie was probably no more than 15, Henry 24. Henry had other royal flings but this affair lasted several years, and Bessie's son, Henry Fitzroy, was given the title Duke of Richmond. Fitzroy's birth may have encouraged Henry to believe it was Catherine's fault his marriage had failed to produce a son. Bastard Richmond could never be king (barring some judicial chicanery), but was a prominent court figure until his death in 1536, probably from tuberculosis.

THE BOLEYN SISTERS

The king's affair with Bessie Blount petered out when Henry's roving eye fell on the two Boleyn sisters. Mary Boleyn, probably the younger by a year or so, had already had a liaison with the King of France. She had married William Carey in 1520 when she may have been as young as 12. In 1526 she bore a son, Henry Carey, who some speculate was the king's child. By then the king had turned his attentions to Mary's sister Anne, perhaps less beautiful than Mary or Bessie, but bewitching – and hard to get. Henry's lust for Anne, and his desire to divorce Catherine in order to marry her, shook the realm. Bessie Blount, meanwhile, had married a baron called Gilbert Tallboys in 1522; after his death she was left a wealthy widow. She remarried, but died in 1540.

EXTORTION

Henry VII's tax collectors Sir Richard Empson and Edmund Dudley successfully filled the royal coffers. But the landed gentry regarded them as crooks – extorting fines, bringing false charges, rigging trials, terrorising juries and lining their own pockets. Henry VIII distanced himself from the scandal by having the tax collectors executed for treason in the second year of his reign.

◄ Henry VIII in his prime, painted by Hans Holbein.

THE BOLEYN AFFAIR

The king's passion for Anne Boleyn was no secret; he named a ship after her and had four love-brooches made by the royal goldsmiths. She would not, however, allow Henry into her bed: it was 'Queen or nothing'. The king must discard his wife.

Henry needed an annulment of his marriage from the Pope in Rome, so he declared an uneasy conscience – he had broken scriptural law by marrying the widow of his dead brother Arthur. Yet muddy waters became cloudier after Catherine said her marriage to Arthur in 1501, when he was 15 and she 16, was never consummated. This was countered by witnesses who remembered hearing Arthur, the morning after the royal couple's 'bedding', boast that all had gone well on the wedding night.

▲ The charges against Anne Boleyn implied that the king had failed to satisfy her lust. It was whispered that Sir Thomas Norris (Groom of the Stool and, therefore, an intimate of Henry) was the father of Anne's daughter, Princess Elizabeth.

THE KING'S GREAT MATTER

In this scandalous atmosphere began the king's 'Great Matter' – the royal divorce. Henry considered promoting his bastard son Richmond over Mary, but Cardinal Wolsey assured the king he could get Rome to agree to a divorce. However, Catherine had powerful relatives who were strongly opposed and Wolsey failed. Failure brought about his downfall; the great cardinal died on his way south to London where a traitor's execution awaited.

Anyone now serving Henry in high office had to be supportive of his all-consuming issue: his divorce and the Church. Those who demurred, like Thomas More, were in trouble. The king was no Protestant, but he had few qualms about taking on the Pope, with the aid of Thomas Cromwell, Chancellor from 1533, who had no loyalty to the Church. Cromwell's lawyers pored over musty documents to find proof that an English king was free from papal jurisdiction. To argue against the king became dangerous. More was beheaded. Bishop John Fisher, a supporter of Queen Catherine, was shot at and one of his servants poisoned by a dish of porridge. The bishop's cook protested it was a joke that backfired, but he himself was boiled to death in a pot. The Abbot of Whitby was charged for calling Anne Boleyn a 'whore'. There was popular support for Catherine, spiced up after Elizabeth Barton, the 'mad maid of Kent', had 'visions' of the Virgin Mary and angels foretelling

➤ Henry VIII and the 'butcher's boy' Cardinal Wolsey; painting by Sir John Gilbert, 1888.

8

evil days should the king put away his wife. Barton's brief celebrity ended in her hanging at Tyburn, but the atmosphere remained feverish, with rumours of plots, portents and accusations that Anne Boleyn was not only a Protestant but had bewitched the king.

➤ A caricature of King Henry VIII leading Anne Boleyn to the Royal Court as Cardinal Wolsey cringes.

STUDIED INSOLENCE

Anne's father Thomas Boleyn (1477–1539) was active in all this diplomatic haggling. As Earl of Wiltshire he was sent to explain the royal divorce to the Emperor Charles V who, as Queen Catherine's nephew, was hard to convince. When Boleyn met the Pope, biased Catholic writers recounted how he insolently declined to kiss the Pope's foot, instead allowing his spaniel to lick it. Boleyn's tasteless humour was also displayed when, giving dinner to the French ambassador shortly after Wolsey's death in 1530, he presented a tableau showing the Cardinal being welcomed into Hell.

DIVORCE, MARRIAGE ...

Henry was not deterred by warnings of a European-wide scandal if he abandoned his wife for Anne, now openly called his 'concubine'. If divorce meant he must rule the Church in England, so be it. He bullied England's bishops and, in May 1533, Archbishop Thomas Cranmer formally ended Henry's marriage to Catherine. By then, the king had at last got Anne to bed. They were married secretly in January 1533, and in September Anne gave birth to a daughter, the future Queen Elizabeth I. Henry had birth notices printed heralding a prince; these were hastily altered to read 'princess' and the disappointed king did not attend the christening.

... DOWNFALL

After Anne suffered two miscarriages, Henry concluded she would not bear the son he needed. His old passion had become a 'cursed and poisoning whore', and he had a new love, Jane Seymour. He wanted Anne out of his life. Surely having had sex with Anne's sister Mary was grounds for annulment? Or was there something stronger? In 1536 the king heard truly scandalous charges: the queen was accused of adultery with five men, including incest with her brother George. Musician Mark Smeaton 'confessed' under torture. The poet Thomas Wyatt and Anne's captain of the king's bodyguards Richard Page were also arrested. It was a sex scandal to rock the realm.

⋀ Mary Boleyn, a one-time mistress of Henry VIII and sister of Anne.

⋁ The Tower of London, where Anne Boleyn was executed in 1536.

The END FOR ANNE

At her trial in May 1536, Anne defended herself bravely but in vain, with Thomas Cromwell pulling the strings and her uncle the Duke of Norfolk presiding. Henry had abandoned her. There were lewd accusations of sodomy and witchcraft, with Anne painted as a treasonable seductress. Even dancing with her brother was evidence of carnal deviance. Guilty verdicts were inevitable. George Boleyn and the other 'adulterers' were beheaded on 17 May. Two days later Anne Boleyn's head was struck off by a swordsman, hired from France, who removed his shoes so the blindfolded queen could not tell from which side he struck; it was the quick death she prayed for. Anne Boleyn was buried in the Chapel of St Peter ad Vincula within the Tower of London. No stone marked her grave.
Mary Boleyn lived in obscurity in Essex until her death in 1543.

SATANIC SEX

Sex outside marriage was officially a crime, for a poor bastard child was an unwelcome burden on a parish; royal bastards fared rather better, however. Homosexuality was illegal if it involved 'unnatural acts' and bestiality (sex with animals) was assumed to be witchcraft. The Anne Boleyn case was sensationalised by allegations of sodomy against the men, implying that the trysts were not only adulterous but demonic and that she had had sex while pregnant.

BEDDING RITES

After a royal marriage a priest would bless the bridal bed, often accompanied by bawdy songs from the guests. The bride was undressed and clad in 'bedding clothes' by attendants, and consummation (witnessed or overheard from outside) might be greeted with cheers and applause. The controversy surrounding the wedding night of Prince Arthur and Catherine of Aragon suggests they at least had some privacy.

➤ A Tudor bed. Royal wedding nights were semi-public, despite the bed-hangings.

ShADOW OF THE SCAFFOLD

Sweet-mannered and virtuous Jane Seymour was betrothed to King Henry the day after Anne Boleyn's execution. They married ten days later. In October 1537 Jane bore Henry a son; Henry now had his legitimate male heir, the future Edward VI, but amid the celebrations the king's 'most entirely beloved wife' died of childbed fever.

ThE GERMAN WIFE

The king's grief was intense; he had lost perhaps his one true love. Thomas Cromwell encouraged a new marriage, for political expediency. Henry unenthusiastically suggested that suitable French women might be brought to Calais for inspection. The French ambassador was scandalised; this was akin to a horseshow – perhaps the king would like to ride each candidate to try them out.

▲ Jane Seymour, loved and then lost.

◀ Anne of Cleves, unloved and paid off.

So Henry chose his fourth wife from a painting by Hans Holbein and on the advice of Cromwell. Anne of Cleves was German, sexually innocent and unprepossessing. Henry was not impressed on first meeting her; he reluctantly went ahead with the wedding in January 1540 but refused to consummate the union. It was all too humiliating and he blamed Cromwell, who paid the price in July: beheaded alongside a notorious 'deviant' as a deliberate humiliation.

▲ Thomas Cromwell, the fixer who was finally condemned.

THE HOWARD SCANDAL

With the Cleves marriage swiftly annulled, Henry took his fifth wife. Catherine Howard was no older than 22 in 1540, while the king was almost 50. Niece to the Duke of Norfolk, and Anne Boleyn's cousin, Catherine had a less-than-pure reputation, soon conveyed to the king by Archbishop Cranmer. She had had sex with her music tutor at 15 and also with Francis Dereham, now her secretary. Dereham protested that at the time of the 'offence' in 1538 he and Catherine had been betrothed (so sex was no sin). Besides, their affair was over – Catherine was now besotted with Thomas Culpepper, a Gentleman of the Privy Chamber. Henry was aghast – Culpepper was a favourite, despite a history of alleged rape and murder. He was doubly betrayed. Catherine, her dancing days over, was confined, her only hope possibly to claim pregnancy. Servants and court ladies provided evidence of secret trysts in the queen's bedroom and even her toilet. Why had Catherine been so reckless? Was her folly down to misery, frustration, or ambition? Henry was ailing, possibly no longer virile, and perhaps Catherine hoped a lover would father the son that would secure her position.

➤ The axe and the block.

THE HUNGERFORD CASE

On the scaffold with Cromwell died Walter, Lord Hungerford, executed for buggery, black magic and supporting the Pilgrimage of Grace religious protest. Hungerford was a troubled soul. His stepmother had been hanged for strangling her first husband, before marrying Walter's father. Walter married three times: his third wife claimed he locked her up and tried to poison her, while having 'unnatural' relations with male staff. On the scaffold in July 1540 Hungerford was reported to be 'rather in a frenzy'. What Cromwell felt can only be imagined.

SHAME AND DISGRACE

When Henry finally accepted the 'evidence' his rage was volcanic – he wept, threatened to take a sword to Catherine and bewailed having married so falsely, so often. Catherine naively denied being betrothed to Dereham, which might have saved her. Her uncle Norfolk abandoned her and she was sent in disgrace to the nunnery at Syon House in Middlesex, stripped of jewels and crown, and then to the Tower, indicted for carnal sin against the king. Culpepper tried to save his own head by accusing Catherine of seducing him, but he and Dereham were executed on 10 December 1541.

Catherine soon shared their fate. The day before her execution she asked to see the axeman's block so she could be shown how to lay her head. She died on the morning of 13 February 1542. Executed with her was Lady Jane Rochford, widow of George Boleyn, for aiding the adultery. Catherine, the king's fifth wife, was buried alongside his second, Anne Boleyn.

CATHERINE'S NARROW ESCAPE

Henry married for the last time in 1543, to the twice-widowed Catherine Parr. The cleverest of his wives, she liked to discuss theology with him, but in June 1546 the king, sick and cantankerous, complained to Bishop Gardiner of Winchester about Catherine's arguing. The bishop said it was scandalous Protestant heresy; Catherine had become a 'serpent' in the royal bosom. An arrest warrant was drawn up, but somehow a copy was left for the queen to see. Catherine hurried to assure Henry that her talk was meant only to ease his pain and to be instructed through his wise replies. They embraced and Henry dismissed the guards sent to arrest her.

HOWARD DOWNFALL

Noble families walked a precarious tightrope. Thomas Howard, Duke of Norfolk, had helped beat the Scots at Flodden in 1513 and was uncle to two queens. Yet he walked into scandal. In the 1520s the duke installed his mistress Elizabeth Holland at his home; the

▲ Catherine Parr (1512–48), Henry VIII's last wife.

duchess claimed she was shut in a room, robbed of her clothes and jewels, manhandled by servants and carted off to Hertfordshire to live on a pittance. Trouble also followed Norfolk's son Henry, Earl of Surrey. Poet and prankster, he was arrogant, moody but seemingly untouchable – Henry VIII loved him and the powerful Duke of Richmond was a close friend. But Surrey was fond of misbehaving: he terrorised the city with a stone-firing crossbow, breaking windows and peppering prostitutes working the riverside taverns; he ate meat during the fast of Lent. Packed off abroad to soldier, he came home in disgrace after a debacle in 1546 against the French near Boulogne.

Norfolk and Surrey's downfall was brought about by Edward and Thomas Seymour, brothers of the king's late wife Jane. The Seymours and Catherine Parr favoured religious reform, while Norfolk was a Catholic. Towards the end of 1546 Henry was persuaded that the Howards were plotting to usurp his throne, and father and son were arrested. Surrey was beheaded in January 1547. Norfolk was saved by the death of the king the day before his planned execution and survived to help secure Mary I's succession in 1553.

FOUR DRUNKS OF THE *MARY ROSE*

On 11 June 1539, the *Mary Rose* was docked in Deptford and four of its crew decided to go ashore and visit a pub. On heading back to the ship after several drinks they realised it had left without them. They found a boat and attempted to catch up with the *Mary Rose*, but due to the strong currents of the Thames, plus the influence of alcohol, they instead collided with a Portuguese merchant vessel, *Saynte John de Cangas*. The four men attempted to board the ship, waking everyone and causing a ruckus. Following an altercation they proceeded to help themselves to the ship's cargo, breaking open three chests and taking rolls of cloth, shirts and a sugar loaf weighing 8lb.

Their haul was later found in the mud of the Thames at Greenwich, where the sailors had obviously decided to dump it. Sadly, there are no surviving records of whether they were found guilty, but the statements seem to show that the mariners admitted they'd done it, albeit while drunk. What sentence was passed will remain a mystery, so we'll probably never know if these four were present when the *Mary Rose* sank six years later.

▲ Geoff Hunt painting of the *Mary Rose* in full sail. (Geoff Hunt, PPRSMA)

THE PERILS OF GLORIANA

Edward VI became king when only 9 years old. Power rested with his uncle Edward Seymour, Duke of Somerset, Regent and Lord Protector of England, until 1552 when the Duke of Northumberland (a former ally) secured his execution for treason. The sickly king pursued religious reform, favouring Protestantism, until dying wretchedly in 1553, probably from tuberculosis.

Northumberland had married his son Guildford Dudley to Lady Jane Grey, a great-granddaughter of Henry VII, and as Edward lay dying the Duke persuaded him to name her queen. Jane lasted only nine days. Edward's sister Mary brushed aside the attempted coup and soon the mob was yelling that Northumberland had poisoned their king. Mary became queen and the duke was beheaded for treason. Lady Jane Grey survived in prison until 1554, when she, her husband and her father were executed following Sir Thomas Wyatt's rebellion against Mary.

THE SEYMOUR AFFAIR

Such events made Princess Elizabeth only too aware of her own pivotally perilous position. Her childhood had been overshadowed by Anne Boleyn's downfall. Tainted as a bastard, shunned by her father and mistrusted by her sister, discretion became second nature. Queen Catherine Parr

▲ The Royal Palace of Hatfield. Although this is the only part of the original building that remains, a short distance from the present Hatfield House, the palace was the childhood home and favourite residence of Queen Elizabeth I.

was kind to her stepdaughter Elizabeth, but after Henry VIII died in 1547 Catherine remarried – her husband (her fourth) was Lord Admiral Thomas Seymour, Somerset's brother. Tall, dark, handsome and dangerously ambitious, he was tempted by the teenaged Elizabeth who was sharing his marital home. He would visit her bedroom, often in his nightshirt, to chase and cuddle. Elizabeth's governess Kat Ashley became alarmed by these 'incontinent' games, when Seymour would 'open the [bed] curtains and ... make as though he would come at her'. Catherine apparently tolerated the 'games' until she found the pair embracing; she then sent Elizabeth away to Hertfordshire. Seymour's arrogance alienated even his brother and he was beheaded in March 1549. Elizabeth had to rebut 'rumours abroad against my honour and modesty', including the 'shameful slander' that she was pregnant with Seymour's child. She was lucky to escape the scandal, and knew it.

◄ The signing of the death warrant of Lady Jane Grey.

SCHEMING DUKE

John Dudley lived dangerously. His father Edmund was executed in 1510; his mother then married Arthur Plantagenet, an illegitimate son of Edward IV. He helped bring down the Howards in 1547. He collected titles: Earl of Warwick, then Duke of Northumberland. His enemies said he forged Edward VI's signature to bring about the execution of Regent Somerset in 1552. After his attempt to make Lady Jane Grey queen collapsed, the scheming duke lost his head for treason on 22 August 1553.

➤ Archbishop Thomas Cranmer, burned at the stake during the reign of Mary I.

MARY AND ELIZABETH

Mary and Elizabeth were never close. Banished from Henry VIII's court after her mother's divorce, Mary felt humiliated by Anne Boleyn. A staunch Catholic, she could not accept divorce or remarriage. After Mary's accession, Elizabeth was sent briefly to the Tower on suspicion of plotting against her sister, but escaped the axe and retired to the country, out of harm's way.

Queen at 37, unwed and dowdy, Mary was shy and did not relish sex, but knew she must marry. She chose Philip, Prince of Spain, meeting him only two days before their wedding in July 1554. By September the queen believed she was pregnant, but the signs proved illusory, and by the late summer of 1555 Philip had departed. Mary still hoped and prayed for a child, even though it was unlikely now, given her age, failing health and absentee spouse.

In her despair religious dogmatism took over. The devout Catholic became 'Bloody Mary', persecuting Protestants: heretics burned at the stake included the elderly Archbishop Cranmer. Suffering from what was probably ovarian cancer, Mary I died in November 1558.

After Elizabeth I's accession, widower Philip swiftly proposed marriage, but she rejected him. 'Gloriana' warily rebuffed all suitors, foreign and domestic, yet her secret love life caused much speculation.

The DUDLEY SCANDAL

Handsome men amused Elizabeth and, as favourites jockeyed for position, gossip and scandal abounded: the queen might be virginal, the court was not. Robert Dudley, later Earl of Leicester, was her 'eyes', possibly her one great love, but already married. On 8 September 1560 Dudley's wife Amy Robsart broke her neck after falling down the stairs at her home near Oxford. The coroner's verdict was misadventure, but Dudley's enemies scented scandal. Was it murder? Had he pushed her so he could marry the queen? Or had William Cecil, the queen's chief minister, had Amy killed to blight Dudley's ambitions? Magistrates were kept busy sentencing scandal-mongers spreading the slander that the queen was pregnant with Dudley's child.

▲ Robert Dudley, Earl of Leicester (1532–88).

Though Dudley's reputation never fully recovered, Elizabeth kept him in her heart; his last letter, written just before his death in 1588, lay in a casket at her bedside.

The GREY GIRL

Tudor marriages often brought trouble. Catherine Grey was the younger sister of the executed Lady Jane Grey (and so of royal lineage), and her husband was Ned, Earl of Hertford, son of Regent Seymour (beheaded in 1552) and nephew of Jane Seymour. Little wonder the pair wed in secret. Queen Elizabeth was outraged and sent the newlyweds to the Tower. Catherine was pregnant, but was unable to prove the marriage, having no papers or witnesses, so her son was declared a bastard. A second son was born in 1563, but Catherine was kept under house arrest until her death in 1568 aged 27. Hertford was released in 1571, on payment of a massive fine: £15,000. He risked two more clandestine marriages, evidently hoping his sons might be legitimised as heirs to the throne, but his hopes were dashed by the accession of James VI of Scotland in 1603.

The RALEIGH AFFAIR

The activities of Elizabeth's naval captains scandalised foreign courts but secretly enriched the queen. Francis Drake, Martin Frobisher and John Hawkins were more at ease on the high seas than at court, but Walter Raleigh was in his element in both – soldier, explorer, writer, wit and all-round show-off. The story of Raleigh spreading his cloak in the mud for the queen to step on may not be true, but it's the kind of thing he might have done.

The queen wanted her favourites to be devoted only to her, but Raleigh married Bess Throckmorton, a maid of honour, in secret, probably in 1591. When a child was born in the spring of 1592, but died, Raleigh and Bess were exposed and in August they were sent to the Tower. Luckily, Raleigh's squadron returned to Plymouth laden with treasure taken from a Portuguese ship and the queen freed him to arrange the payout. Raleigh outlived Elizabeth but spent thirteen years in the Tower during the reign of James I, and was beheaded in 1618 after leading a disastrous raid to the Caribbean. The devoted Bess was said to have kept her husband's embalmed head until her death in the 1640s.

▲ Frobisher, Hawkins and Drake.

SECRETS OF THE BEDROOM

Tudor ideals of feminine beauty were white skin and fair hair, a high, smooth forehead, thin eyebrows and red lips. Women bleached their hair in the sun, but shaded their faces with masks. Some cosmetics were highly toxic (white lead mixed with vinegar). Blackened teeth were further damaged by scrubbing with a powdered pumice stone, brick and coral. A Tudor lady rarely bathed, using scented pomanders to mask body odours.

▼ A ship sailing past the Tower of London on a stained-glass window at the early medieval church of All Hallows by the Tower, London.

WEBS OF INTRIGUE

Elizabeth I was threatened by internal unrest, mad-eyed assassins and foreign plots, but protected by a web of spies, agents and informers, set up to snare conspirators. A prime target for the queen's intelligence chief, Sir Francis Walsingham, was Elizabeth's Scottish cousin.

THE SCOTTISH QUEEN

Mary Queen of Scots was crowned at Stirling Castle in 1543, at just 9 months old. She was in line to be Queen of England after the children of Henry VIII, but she was Catholic. Mary might have been Queen of France, had not her husband Francis, heir to the throne, died. A young widow, she returned in 1561 to Scotland, a country she barely knew and in the grip of religious reformation led by John Knox, a Protestant zealot whom Mary came to dislike almost as much as Scotland's winters.

THE RIZZIO MURDER

In 1565 Mary married Henry Stuart, Lord Darnley, who, like her, was a grandchild of Margaret Tudor, sister of Henry VIII. She became pregnant but Darnley's actions were selfish and ambitious. Starved of affection, Mary liked to play cards with her Italian secretary David Rizzio and recall happier times in France. Darnley's vanity was outraged, and in March 1566 he arranged Rizzio's brutal murder in the queen's rooms at Holyroodhouse in Edinburgh. In June, Mary gave birth to a son, James, but she never forgave Darnley.

▲ Elizabeth I's reign was rarely free of plot and counter-plot.

THE SPY GAME

Tudor espionage was conducted in the best 'cloak and dagger' tradition. Coded letters written in milk or lemon juice were read by warming over a candle. Messages were hidden in the bungs of wine-casks, inside the heels of shoes, in false-bottomed boxes or stuffed into men's codpieces. Agents met informants in taverns wearing disguises and infiltrated conspiracies by pretending to be assassins.

DARNLEY AND BOTHWELL

On the night of 10 February 1567, Mary was awoken by an explosion. Gunpowder had blown up the house at Kirk o'Field where Darnley was recuperating after sickness and he was found dead in the garden – half-naked and strangled – beside a servant, also dead. The chief suspect was James Hepburn, Earl of Bothwell, whom Mary had consulted about a possible divorce. Bothwell was cleared of Darnley's murder, but by now he had made powerful enemies. In April 1567 he 'abducted' Mary to his castle at Dunbar, allegedly 'ravishing her'. In May the couple married.

The scandalised Scottish nobles now rose up against Mary; Bothwell retreated and left Mary to her fate. She was forced to abdicate in favour of her infant son James. After imprisonment and escape, a possible miscarriage of twins and defeat at Langside near Glasgow, she fled to England. Bothwell fled into exile and became insane, dying in Denmark in 1578.

⌃ Mary Queen of Scots, who was beheaded at Fotheringhay Castle in 1587. Painting by Philippe Jacques van Bree, 1819.

⌃ The murder of David Rizzio, arranged in 1566 by the Scottish queen's husband, Lord Darnley, and his group of conspirators, who stabbed him sixty times.

MARY AND ELIZABETH

Mary was an uninvited, unwelcome guest in England. Elizabeth did not want to send her back to Scotland, but a free Mary might take the crown, especially after Elizabeth was excommunicated by the Pope in 1570, leaving any Catholic lawfully able to remove her. For eighteen years Mary was trapped in a web of conspiracy. Plot after plot was uncovered, as double agent Gilbert Gifford passed Mary's secret letters on to his boss Walsingham.

WHO KILLED MARLOWE?

The Catholic Church regarded Elizabeth I as heretical; atheist playwright Christopher Marlowe was most certainly destined for hellfire. Born the same year as Shakespeare (1564), Marlowe was far more publicly scandalous than the bard of Avon. Cambridge-educated, he was a street brawler, probably homosexual, and almost certainly a government agent. In May 1593 he was stabbed in a fight at a house in Deptford. The killer, Ingram Frizer, claimed self-defence and was pardoned. Had the secret service terminated Marlowe for crossing the line?

➤ A portrait, supposedly of Christopher Marlowe, 1585.

THE RIDOLFI PLOT

Italian banker Roberto Ridolfi backed the Catholic cause financially and through his many contacts in England and abroad. He supported a plan to stage an uprising against Elizabeth, assassinate her if necessary, and make Mary queen, with the new Duke of Norfolk (Surrey's son) as king. Aware that he was being spied on, Ridolfi slipped over to the Low Countries to plot invasion with Spanish army commanders. Three enciphered letters sent by him to contacts in England, including Norfolk, were intercepted when the courier was arrested at Dover. Convinced Ridolfi was a real threat, the security service opened more of his letters and arrested Norfolk, who was beheaded in 1572. Ridolfi managed to stay out of reach and died in Italy in 1612.

THE THROCKMORTON CONSPIRACY

Francis Throckmorton, a Catholic, was another conspirator aiming to replace Elizabeth with Mary Queen of Scots. In Throckmorton's London house, Walsingham's agents found lists of Catholic insurgents and harbour plans to guide an invasion army. Spanish ambassador Bernardino de Mendoza was implicated, and Henry Percy, 8th Earl of Northumberland, was found to have hosted a meeting at Petworth to discuss a landing by French soldiers. When this was revealed under torture by a witness, Percy was marched to the Tower; Mendoza fled the country. In July 1584 Throckmorton was executed at Tyburn.

A year later, on 21 June 1585, Percy was found dead in his cell, shot through the heart. Was it suicide or murder? Catholics suspected murder, since the previous day a new gaoler had taken charge of the prisoner, on the orders of Elizabeth's minister Christopher Hatton.

MARY'S DOWNFALL

While Elizabeth survived several near-misses by assassins, Mary remained a prisoner until 1586, when Walsingham secured evidence to convict her of treason. Unaware that his friend Robin Poley was a government agent, Catholic plotter Anthony Babington had written to Mary. To her intercepted

▲ Queen Elizabeth I consented, reluctantly, to the execution of Mary Queen of Scots in 1587.

reply, agents added a forged request for the names of conspirators. Babington duly supplied a list and thus was caught – a gleeful code-breaker in Walsingham's office doodled a gallows on the sheet of paper. Babington and his fellow conspirators were executed as traitors (hanged, drawn and quartered) and Elizabeth reluctantly signed Mary's death warrant, though she later insisted Mary's execution on 8 February 1587 was against her will. Catholic courts across Europe expressed outrage, but there was mute protest from Scotland. Mary's son James VI, already confirmed as Elizabeth's heir, was not going to rock the boat.

◄ Mary Queen of Scots, about to go to her death. Painting by Philippe Jacques van Bree, 1819.

PIRATES AND PRIVATEERS

The 15th and 16th centuries were a time of world-changing naval exploration. In 1492 Christopher Columbus set sail from Europe to America and thus changed the course of world history. Sir Francis Drake was an Elizabethan sailor and navigator and became the first Englishman to circumnavigate the globe. Walter Raleigh also took to the seas and sponsored the first English colony in America. All this traffic on the seas meant piracy could be a lucrative enterprise. Many pirates had served in merchant or naval ships prior to turning to piracy. As pirates they hoped to become rich on the plunders of treasure and cargo ships. As a privateer (a lawful pirate) Francis Drake would attack Spanish treasure ships returning from the New World and share his profits with Elizabeth I.

SCANDALS AT SEA

Seafaring was a risky business. Many Tudor ships simply vanished somewhere beyond the horizon, never to be seen again. Wooden sailing ships, incredibly small to our eyes (in 1583 Humphrey Gilbert was lost trying to sail back from North America in the 10-ton *Squirrel*), crossed oceans relying on basic navigation instruments, the wind and currents. Seamen ate rotten food and drank foul water, and sailed in fear of sea monsters, storms, savages and the vengeful Spanish. Spain guarded its New World jealously and treated captive Protestants harshly. The noblemen and merchants who sponsored these piratical voyages seldom knew the dangers. The queen herself was a silent partner, sponsoring ships and taking her share of the profits.

SECRET VOYAGES

Many Tudor voyages were secret and included military raids, piratical expeditions and covert explorations of new seaways and possible colonies. Spain saw the 'seadogs' as criminal heretics and captured English mariners could expect marooning, flogging, galley-slavery and burning as heretics. Despite the dangers, the lure of gold and adventure drew nobleman and commoner alike. The Earl of Leicester's illegitimate son Sir Robert Dudley was a navigator, and George Clifford, Earl of Cumberland, a royal favourite, made a dozen voyages from 1586.

◄ The English arrive in the New World. Engraving by Theodor de Bry, 1590.

➤ The Battle of Lepanto in 1571, in which Tudor anti-hero Thomas Stucley took part.

◄ Christopher Columbus bidding farewell to the Queen of Spain on his departure for the New World, 3 August 1492.

A TUDOR ADVENTURER

Of chequered Tudor careers, few were more scandalous than Thomas Stucley's. Born about 1525 in Devon, he went off to France, became a spy and, on returning to England, became a double agent; he ended up disowned and in jail. Emerging disgruntled and in debt, Stucley contrived to marry a London heiress, but he squandered her money and, after being charged with 'coining' (forgery), took to piracy. His fortunes turned after he successfully entertained Queen Elizabeth with a staged naval battle on the Thames, and he proposed setting up a colony in Florida, with the queen providing one of six ships. Nevertheless, his continued piracy and failure in the venture caused her to disown him, so he turned rebel-traitor, offering to lead a Spanish-backed invasion of Ireland. In this expedition, too, he failed: the ships provided were so rotten that he never made it. Turning his back on Britain, he fought at the sea battle in Lepanto against the Turks in 1571 and joined a Portuguese expedition to Morocco, where he was killed in 1578. His misadventures became so well known that they were sung in London's streets by ballad-sellers.

SINGEING THE BEARD

Francis Drake was a typical Tudor blend of bravery and ruthlessness – during his round-the-world voyage he hanged Thomas Doughty for mutiny and witchcraft, even though Doughty was close to Drake's government sponsor Christopher Hatton. In 1587 Drake, fervently anti-Catholic, led an attack on the port of Cadiz, setting sail for Spain before the cautious Elizabeth could countermand his orders. The English burned more than two dozen Spanish vessels and on the voyage home seized a Spanish bullion-ship. Since England and Spain were not officially at war, Spain was outraged, and having 'his beard singed' made King Philip determined on revenge: the Armada sailed the next year. Its defeat was an English triumph and the queen could look forward to more rich pickings – a single Spanish prize cargo paid her expenses for a year.

HEROES DIE AT ODDS

Devon men John Hawkins and Francis Drake were giants of Tudor ocean exploration, but to the Spanish they were instruments of the Devil. Having sailed together off and on since the 1560s, the two seadogs perished within weeks of one another, quarrelling during an expedition to the Caribbean. Hawkins died in November 1595, 'despairing of the venture'; Drake, 'sick of the flux', followed in January 1596.

THE FALL OF ESSEX

Tudor egos often clashed violently. In 1596 an Anglo-Dutch fleet sailed secretly to attack Spain. Its co-commanders included the volatile Earl of Essex, Raleigh and Howard of Effingham; among the volunteers was the poet John Donne. Despite furious rows, the raid succeeded: Cadiz was burned and the victors sacked Faro in Portugal, making off with the bishop's library – which found a new home in Oxford, in the Bodleian Library collection. In the 1590s, Essex was the ageing queen's most glamorous favourite, but his downfall was spectacular. Elizabeth sent him to Ireland, where the Irish rebels ran rings around his army, to the glee of his rivals. Returning in disgrace, Essex gathered hothead support (one friend was Robert Catesby, later a Gunpowder plotter). He marched through London, apparently convinced the city would back his bid for supreme power. This folly cost him his life. Elizabeth was tired of his preening and Essex was beheaded for treason on 25 February 1601.

ARMADA AFTERMATH

In the Armada battles of 1588 the Elizabethan navy lost not one ship. However, hundreds of Armada veterans died in England after the event. Their commander, Lord Howard, complained of the 'sickness and mortality amongst us' – he was writing from Margate, where he saw sailors dying in the street, their only shelter 'barns and such outhouses'. It was outrageous that, penniless and barely clothed, 'them that have served so valiantly should die so miserably'.

> Sir Francis Drake.

▲ Vintage engraving (1883) of the Spanish Armada in the English Channel in 1588.

THE ROANOKE MYSTERY

In 1585 Raleigh sent 108 men to Roanoke Island off North Carolina – England's first colony in America. The first colonists soon went home, but in 1587 more landed there: 91 men, 17 women and 9 children. On 18 August 1587 Eleanor, wife of Ananias Dare and daughter of expedition leader John White, had a baby, named Virginia. When White sailed for fresh supplies, the Dares and others stayed behind. White did not return until 1590 (after the Armada), by which time the colonists had vanished. One theory is that they went to live with nearby Croatoan Indians.

➤ Portrait of Sir Walter Raleigh, now in the North Carolina Museum of History.

SEX, SIN AND DEVILRY

Most Tudor scandals had sex and religion at their heart, with money close behind. As the Protestant Reformation took root across Europe, radical ideas, such as the suggestion by Polish astronomer Copernicus (1473–1543) that the earth moved around the sun (and was not therefore the centre of God's universe), shook convictions.

STRIPPING THE CHURCH

While many churchmen were poor, Cardinal Wolsey managed to build a palace at Hampton Court fit for a prince, gifting it to Henry VIII. After the king made himself head of the English Church by the Act of Supremacy of 1534, the Spanish ambassador said scornfully that English bishops were 'of less account than shoemakers'. As Protestant preachers railed against Church corruption and 'popishness', Thomas Cromwell asset-stripped the monasteries; Henry VIII was cash-strapped, so this plunder was

▲ Hampton Court Palace, where Henry VIII and Anne Boleyn spent their honeymoon.

welcome. From the 1540s religious persecution increased, with strife between Protestants and Catholics leading to torture, hangings and burnings.

ANNE ASKEW

In June 1546 Anne Askew was charged with heresy, for denying that the sacramental bread and wine were the body and blood of Christ. She had been thrown out by her husband for causing such scandal and now faced torture on the rack. When Anthony Knyvett, Lieutenant of the Tower, protested that racking a woman was illegal, her interrogators took over. Still resolute, but unable to walk, she was carried in a chair to the stake; a gunpowder charge set in the fire cut short her agonies.

THE CATHOLIC UNDERGROUND

Burnings became only too common in the reign of Mary I, when Protestant victims included the 'Oxford martyrs', bishops Ridley and Latimer, in 1555, and, as mentioned earlier, Archbishop Cranmer. Though Elizabeth I was less dogmatic, religion remained a controversial area of public and private life. Catholics faced discrimination and were seen as agents of the enemy, Spain. Catholics who did not recant were driven to worship in secret: Catholic priests arriving to 'reconvert' England conducted mass in private chapels and hid in 'priest holes' in Catholic homes. If captured they faced torture and death, as did laypeople prepared to die for their beliefs – like Margaret Clitherow. A butcher's wife living in York, she was accused of going to mass and hiding Catholic priests. Stripped naked, she was laid across a sharp stone and had crushing weights loaded onto her chest; she was dead in a quarter of an hour.

DEVILS, DEMONS AND WITCHES

For most people in the Tudor age the Devil was real, waiting to tempt the weak into sin and damnation. His agents were witches and demons. Eccentric, confused old women risked being branded 'witch'. Superstition was rife. A bridegroom finding a piece

A man being tortured on the rack.

Archbishop Cranmer tried to avoid execution by recanting his support of Protestantism, but he was nevertheless sentenced to be burnt to death in 1556. He therefore thrust his right hand, with which he had signed his recantation, into the fire first.

of knotted leather in his bed feared a jealous rival or jilted lover was trying to make him impotent. A French demonologist warned that Europe harboured almost two million witches, multiplying 'as worms in a garden'.

A sensational Tudor witch scandal occurred in 1593 in East Anglia, involving the five daughters of Robert Throckmorton, who became ill, apparently with fits. The girls accused one Alice Samuel of bewitching them. Alice was also accused of causing the death of Lady Cromwell, who had imagined herself tormented to death by a devil-cat. Consequently Alice Samuel, her husband and their daughter Agnes were hanged at Huntingdon. Explanations, apart from hysteria, include the suggestion that the girls were affected by ergotism, a form of poisoning from eating contaminated rye bread.

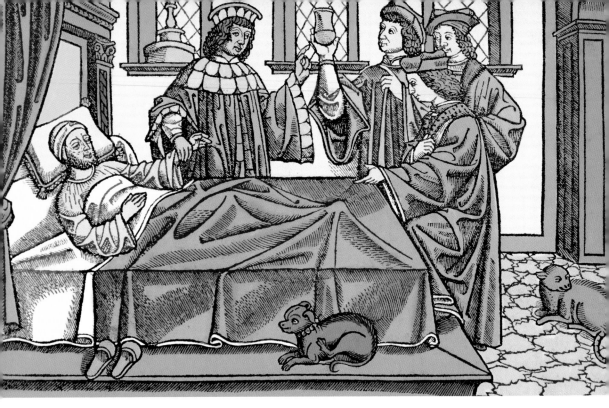

▲ Doctors with a patient in the 16th century.

LONDON'S DARK SECRETS

London was a visible emblem of devilry for many Puritans, a city seething with scandal and iniquity. The age was degenerate: historian John Stow (1525–1605) called it 'the most scoffing, respectless and unthankful age that ever was'. The country visitor was shocked, or enticed, by London's vices: bear-pits and cockfights, theatres, taverns and brothels. There were perils, of course: syphilis ('Spanish pox' or 'the French welcome') had been affecting Europeans since the 1490s, brought over from the New World. It was just one of many health fears. Women feared pregnancy, birth and childbed fever. Children died tragically young from a range of complaints and the 'sweating sickness' killed with terrifying suddenness. Plague returned periodically, closing theatres and driving those who could to the country to escape 'the black pestilence'.

THE MAGICAL MATHEMATICIAN

The most guarded secrets were those of alchemy. William Cecil, Lord Burghley, invested in a company offering to turn iron into gold, and one of the most misunderstood Tudor scientists was John Dee (1527–1608), who dabbled in alchemy. Soon after Queen Mary's accession in 1553, Dee was accused of plotting to remove her by poison or magic. He talked his way out of trouble, and when Elizabeth became queen he was consulted about a propitious day for her coronation. Dee gave advice to explorers and explained the new geography to the queen. He was in favour of the new calendar, introduced by Pope Gregory XIII in 1582, but Protestant bishops opposed any change and the Gregorian calendar was shelved in England for 170 years.

Dee claimed to have 'transmuted' to gold a piece of metal cut from a warming pan, which he sent to the queen to show how the gold fitted the hole. In 1583 a mob vandalised his house. He and his friend Edward Kelly were said to have conjured spirits using a magic mirror, while Kelly persuaded Dee they should share wives. When Dee appealed to James I to clear his name of slander, the new king, terrified of magic, declined and the magical mathematician died penniless

in 1608, selling most of his books to support his family. Perhaps like Prospero, in Shakespeare's *The Tempest*, he should have sought refuge on an island.

JEWS AND MUSLIMS

To be an atheist was scandalous in Tudor times; to be Jewish only slightly less so. Jews had been expelled from England in the 1200s but were 'readmitted' in 1494, with most arrivals being 'conversos' (Portuguese or Spanish converts to Christianity). Converso Dr Roderigo Lopez, physician to Elizabeth I, was executed in 1594, probably on false evidence, for conspiracy against the queen. Depictions of Jews in Shakespeare's *The Merchant of Venice* and Marlowe's *The Jew of Malta* were unfavourable. Christian Europe and the Muslim world, led by the Ottomans and the Moguls in India, were frequently at odds, but Muslim galley-slaves freed from Spanish ships were granted asylum in England, and they and 'Moorish' traders were to be seen around London or the ports.

◀ John Dee, man of mystery and modern ideas.

⩑ Nostradamus (1503–66), French astrologer, doctor and prophet.

NOSTRADAMUS AND THE NEWS

In 1555 French astrologer-chemist Michel de Notredame, better known as Nostradamus, published *Centuries*, a book of predictions of future events. It caused a sensation: some thought he was a servant of evil, or just mad, while others believed his prophecies came from God. Nobility came to him for advice; one admirer of his was Catherine de Medici, the queen consort of King Henry II of France. Nostradamus was said to have even predicted his own death. After years of suffering from gout and then dropsy, on 1 July 1566 he is alleged to have told his secretary Jean de Chavigny, 'You will not find me alive by sunrise.' The next morning he was indeed dead.

PLACES TO VISIT

There are a number of historic buildings that survive from the Tudor era, plus many other places with links to the people and events of the time. Below is a selection of places worth a visit. Many have their own stories, both secret and scandalous, and most surviving buildings are grand, reflecting the lives of the rich and powerful rather than those of ordinary people. Visitor attractions featuring dungeons, torture instruments, execution relics and medical horrors provide grisly reminders of the darker side of Tudor life.

Anne of Cleves House
52 Southover High St, Lewes, East Sussex, BN7 1JA
www.sussexpast.co.uk/properties-to-discover/anne-of-cleves-house

Burghley House
Stamford, Lincolnshire, PE9 3JY
www.burghley.co.uk

Eltham Palace
Eltham, London, SE9 5QE
www.english-heritage.org.uk/daysout/properties/eltham-palace-and-gardens

Globe Theatre, London
21 New Globe Walk, Bankside, London, SE1 9DT
www.shakespearesglobe.com

Haddon Hall
Bakewell, Derbyshire, DE45 1LA
www.haddonhall.co.uk

Hampton Court Palace
East Molesey, Surrey, KT8 9AU
www.hrp.org.uk/hamptoncourtpalace

Hardwick Hall
Chesterfield, Derbyshire, S44 5QL
www.nationaltrust.org.uk/hardwick

Hatfield House
Hatfield Park, Hatfield, Hertfordshire, AL9 5NQ
www.hatfield-house.co.uk

Hever Castle
Hever Road, Hever, Kent, TN8 7NG
www.hevercastle.co.uk

Kenilworth Castle
Castle Green, Kenilworth, Warwickshire, CV8 1NE
www.english-heritage.org.uk/Kenilworth

Longleat House
Warminster, Wiltshire, BA12 7NW
www.longleat.co.uk/explore/longleathouse

Mary Rose Museum
Portsmouth Historic Dockyard, Main Rd, Portsmouth, PO1 3PY
www.historicdockyard.co.uk/maryrose

Montacute House
Yeovil, Somerset, TA15 6XP
www.nationaltrust.org.uk/montacute-house

National Maritime Museum
Park Row, Greenwich, London, SE10 9NF
www.rmg.co.uk/national-maritime-museum

Palace of Holyroodhouse
Edinburgh, EH8 8DX
www.royalcollection.org.uk/visit/palace-of-holyrood-house

Rievaulx Abbey
North Yorkshire, YL6 5LB
www.english-heritage.org.uk/daysout/properties/rievaulx-abbey

Shakespeare's Birthplace
Henley St, Stratford-upon-Avon, CV37 6QW
www.shakespeare.org.uk/home

Tower of London
London, EC3N 4AB
www.hrp.org.uk/TowerOfLondon

Wilton House
Wilton, Salisbury, SP2 0BJ
www.wiltonhouse.com

Winchester Cathedral
Hampshire, SO23 9LS
www.winchester-cathedral.org.uk

◄ The Elizabethan garden at Kenilworth Castle.